From:

THE GIFT FOR
GIRLS

Contributors: Sally Norton, Sally Jeffrie,
Gemma Reece, Juliana Foster
and Tracey Turner

Illustrations by Katy Jackson,
Amanda Enright and Nellie Ryan

THE GIFT FOR GIRLS

Michael O'Mara Books Limited

The Gift For Girls includes material from *The Girls' Book*, *The Girls' Book Two*, *The Girls' Book Three*, *The Girls' Book of Glamour* and *The Girls' Book of Secrets* published in 2007, 2008 and 2009 by Buster Books.

First published in Great Britain in 2009 by Buster Books, an imprint of Michael O'Mara Books Limited, 9 Lion Yard, Tremadoc Road, London SW4 7NQ

A CIP catalogue record for this book is available from the British Library.

ISBN: 978-1-84317-424-0

10 9 8 7 6 5 4 3 2 1

www.mombooks.com/busterbooks

Printed and bound in China by WKT

CONTENTS

HOW TO MAKE ICE CREAM FROM SNOW

Forget building snowmen. When a flurry of the white stuff starts to fall, it means only one thing – pudding!

You Will Need:

- a cup of full fat milk – icy cold
- ½ a teaspoon of vanilla essence (optional) • ½ a cup of sugar
- four or five cups of CLEAN snow

WHAT YOU DO

1. Collect your snow from outside in a clean bowl.

2. Bring the snow into your house and pop it in the freezer.

3. Mix together the milk, sugar and vanilla essence and stir until the sugar dissolves in the milk.

4. Slowly add spoonfuls of snow to the mixture. Stir it constantly until it's as thick as normal ice cream.

HOW TO MAKE YOUR OWN LIPGLOSS

1. Put a tablespoon of petroleum jelly in a microwaveable container. Heat it gently for half a minute to soften it.

2. Place a teaspoon of hot water into a bowl. Add in some raspberry- or strawberry-flavoured powdered drink mix, a tiny amount at a time, stirring constantly, until no more of the mix dissolves in the water.

3. Add the coloured water to the petroleum jelly one drop at a time, until you get the colour you want.

4. Pour your mixture into a small, clean pot and allow it to cool.

HOW TO MAKE A COMPASS

Here's a method of making a simple compass. Pick a flat leaf and allow it to float on the surface of a cup that is full of water.

Holding the eye of a sewing needle, wipe the point down the side of a magnet. Repeat about 50 times. Make sure that you stroke the magnet in one direction only. This has the effect of magnetizing the needle.

Carefully lay the needle on the top of the leaf, and watch as the leaf slowly turns. The needle will eventually line up along the line of the Earth's North and South Magnetic Poles, with its tip pointing north.

HOW TO MAKE A BOAT IN A NUTSHELL

If you crack a walnut really carefully, the shell will break into two perfect halves. Transform them into boats that will float on water.

Cut a rectangle of paper to create the sail. You can decorate it if you like. Thread a cocktail stick through it to form a mast.

Push a small lump of modelling clay into the middle of the walnut half. Push one end of the cocktail stick into the modelling clay.

Grab a friend and head off to the nearest stream.

HOW TO CATCH A SPIDER

If you'd rather not share your room with a spider, check out how to capture it for long enough to transfer it elsewhere.

• If the spider's loitering on a wall or windowsill, just place a clear glass tumbler over the top. Slide a piece of stiff card under the rim. You can now carry the spider safely out to the garden and release it.

• If the spider has spun a web, you'll need to hold the glass underneath – spiders tend to drop down from their webs when they sense danger. Again, seal it inside the glass with a piece of card.

• If a spider's crawling high up, try catching it on a feather duster. Once you've caught it, tip it into a glass and seal with card.

HOW TO BE A MATHS MAGICIAN

Ask your friends to try this simple sum. Read it out just as it appears opposite. Don't let your friends use a pencil and paper or a calculator – they must figure it out in their heads.

Your friends will probably say the answer to the sum is 5,000.

Take 1,000 and add 40 to it.
Now add another 1,000.
Now add 30.
Now add another 1,000.
Now add 20.
Add another 1,000.
Finally, add 10.

What's the total?

Congratulations, you are a maths magician, because this is the wrong answer. The right answer is 4,100.

If your friends don't believe you, make them do the sum again using a calculator as you read the instructions aloud.

HOW TO MAKE YOUR OWN POM-POMS

Cheerleaders hold a pom-pom in each hand. You can buy these in a toy shop, but it is so much more fun to make your own.

You Will Need:

- ten plastic bags per pom-pom
- a ruler • scissors • a felt-tip pen

WHAT YOU DO

1. Smooth each bag out flat. Use a ruler and pen to draw a line 30 cm above the base of the bag and parallel to it.

2. Cut along the line, removing the part of the bag with the handles.

3. Starting at the open end, cut about 20 cm down the depth of the bag, stopping 10 cm from the bottom. Repeat across the whole width of the bag to form strips about 2 cm wide.

4. Repeat this with all the bags.

5. Gather the prepared bags, holding them at the uncut bases. To make a handle for your pom-pom, scrunch the bases together and secure by wrapping a long strip of sticky tape around them or use a strong elastic band. Finally, rub the finished pom-poms between your hands to fluff them up.

HOW TO EXPLAIN WHY YOU ARE LATE FOR SCHOOL

It's always a good idea to have a few excuses up your sleeve should you ever be late for school (through no fault of your own, of course).

'I came all the way to school before I realized I still had my pyjamas on, and had to go home and change.'

'When I got here my teacher wasn't in the classroom, so I went out looking for her.'

'I was abducted by aliens for experimental purposes. I have been gone for 50 years, but fortunately in Earth time it was only an hour.'

'I invented a time machine that took me forward to my exam results. I saw that I get straight As, so I thought I might as well take things easy from now on.'

'I was helping Little Bo Peep find her sheep.'

'I squeezed the toothpaste too hard, and spent all morning getting it back in the tube.'

'My parents lost the keys to my cage.'

'I can't tell you why I'm late. The Government has sworn me to secrecy.'

'I'm not late . . . everyone else is early.'

'I had a dream and I was top of the class, so I didn't bother getting out of bed.'

HOW TO MAKE A SECRET BOOK SAFE

Do you need a top-secret hiding place for your diary? Here's an old classic you could try. It's time to get seriously sneaky . . .

You Will Need:

• an old hardback book that is bigger and thicker than your diary (have a look in your local charity shop for the oldest-looking one you can find)

• a sheet of card • scissors

1. Draw a rectangle on a piece of card, 2 cm smaller on each side than the size of a page in the book. Cut it out to make your template.

2. Open the book near the beginning and fold three or four pages in half, as shown. Place your template on top of the folded pages and draw round it.

3. Now cut the folded pages along the outline you have drawn.

4. Repeat steps 2 and 3 until there are only a few intact pages left of your book. Place your diary inside the hole in your book and close the cover.

5. Put your fake book on a shelf among all the others – no one will have any idea what is inside it.

HOW TO TELL IF SOMEONE HAS READ YOUR DIARY

Have you ever suspected someone has been reading your diary? Here are some tricks you can use to catch sneaky snoopers out.

Not A Hair Out Of Place. Take one of your hairs – you will find tons in your hairbrush. Tuck one end of it between the cover of your diary and the first page. Tuck the other end between the last page and the back cover. Pop your diary in its usual hiding place. Next time you look, the hair should still be in place. If it isn't, you know somebody has been nosing around where they're not welcome.

A Powdery Plot. Sprinkle some talcum powder onto the last page you have written on in your diary. Only sprinkle a tiny amount, so that it is hardly noticeable. Close the diary and go about your business. If someone has been snooping, the next time you look, you'll notice that the powder has fallen onto the floor near your diary's hiding place.

Suggestions For Snoopers. Write a false entry in your diary. If, for example, you think it is your little brother who is reading your diary, write something like, 'If [Ben] would buy me some sweets from the shop every now and then, I would definitely let him use my computer.' If your brother miraculously starts buying you sweets, you're on to him.

HOW TO LOOK BEAUTIFUL TOMORROW

Want to look fab but can't be bothered with lengthy beauty routines? Simple – just boost your looks while you're tucked up in bed. You'll look beautiful in the morning.

Get Prettier Feet. There's no need to scrub away at dry heels and hard skin for hours. Simply slather on lots of thick body lotion, pull on some cotton socks and head for bed. You'll wake up to much softer feet.

Get Smoother Lips. Slick chapped lips with petroleum jelly before bed. In the morning, rub gently with a clean, damp flannel to remove any flakes of dead skin.

Get Softer Hands. Apply a dollop of hand cream straight after washing your hands – it'll seal in extra moisture and work wonders on hands and nails while you dream.

Get Shinier Hair. For the glossiest locks ever, just smooth lots of thick conditioner on to freshly shampooed hair before bedtime. Protect your

pillow by covering it with an old towel. Rinse and style your hair in the morning.

Get Clearer Skin. Don't worry about that spot ruining your day. Just dot on some tea-tree oil before bed – it's the best pimple buster known to girl-kind.

HOW TO WIN A BET

Make a bet with your friends that they cannot fold a piece of paper in half more than seven times. It sounds easy, but no matter how big the piece of paper, it is impossible to do. Feel free to promise your friends anything if they succeed. Don't worry – they won't.

HOW TO EAT A GOLDFISH

You don't really have to eat a goldfish. This is a great trick and is bound to cause quite a stir. All you need is a goldfish bowl filled with water containing a thin slice of carrot cut into the shape of a goldfish.

WHAT YOU DO

1. Stand between your friend and the bowl. Discreetly turn away from her and swirl the water in the bowl with your fingers. This will make the carrot 'goldfish' appear to swim.

2. Turn back and announce you're feeling peckish. Your pal may suggest a biscuit or a piece of fruit. Refuse politely, telling her you have a perfect high-protein snack to hand.

3. Plunge your hand into the bowl and pull out the 'fish'. Bounce it around in your palm a bit to make it look as though it's flapping around.

4. Pop the carrot into your mouth, crunch it, and swallow. Smile sweetly and leave the room, while your friend opens and closes her mouth in horror, looking a bit like ... well, a goldfish!

HOW TO REMOVE A RING THAT IS STUCK

If you ever try on a friend's ring that's too small and it gets stuck, don't panic – just follow these steps.

Step One: Cool It. Fill a bowl with cold water and tip in a tray of ice. Hold your hand in the ice water for ten seconds. This will help take down any swelling in your finger.

Step Two: Oil It. Rub plenty of hand cream, olive oil or washing-up liquid in and around the ring and up the length of your finger.

Step Three: Twist It. Gently twist the ring, as you slowly work it up and over the knuckle of your finger.

HOW TO TALK LIKE A SURFER GIRL

Learn some essential 'surf speak', and convince people you're a bona fide surfer girl.

The Deck. The bit of the surfboard you stand on.

Carve A Wave. This is a classic surfing move where you make wiggly turns when surfing on a wave.

Impact Zone. The place where the waves are breaking.

The Soup. The white foamy water created when a wave has broken.

Stink Eye. A mean stare normally given when another surfer's done something bad, like dropping into your wave.

Tube. This is when a wave breaks over the top of you so you're surfing inside a cylindrical hole – all surfers dream about it.

Green Room. The inside of a tube.

Grommet. A young surfer.

Wipeout. This is where you fall off your surfboard in spectacular style!

HOW TO PLAY WINK MURDER

Wink Murder is the perfect spooky game for Halloween or a sleepover.

HOW TO PLAY

Grab at least four friends and sit in a circle. Deal one playing card face down for each person who is playing – one of the cards must be the Ace of Spades.

Each player looks at their card (without showing it to anyone else). The person who has the Ace of Spades is the Murderer!

The players sit in silence, looking at each other. The Murderer kills a victim by winking at her without anyone else noticing. When a player has been winked at she must 'die'. She can scream dramatically or just slump in her chair – so long as she makes it clear to the other players that she is dead.

The Murderer wins if she 'kills' all the other players. She loses if someone spots her and correctly accuses her of being the Murderer before everyone is 'dead'.

HOW TO MAKE YOUR OWN LUXURY BUBBLE BATH

Here's a quick and simple way to make some luxurious bubble bath that you can enjoy when treating yourself to a well-deserved pampering session. Alternatively, put some in a pretty glass bottle and give it to your best friend as a present.

1. In a clean bowl, mix together two cups of clear or light-coloured shampoo, three cups of water and two teaspoons of salt. Stir the mixture gently until it thickens slightly.

2. Pour a tiny amount of red food colouring into your mixture and stir again. Keep adding the food colouring until the mixture is a perfect pink colour.

3. Add ten drops of an essential oil for a wonderful scent. Rose, lavender, ylang-ylang, sandalwood, marjoram, myrrh, rosewood and camomile have relaxing and luxurious scents.

4. Pour the bubble bath into a bottle and seal.

HOW TO MAKE YOUR OWN HERBAL TEA

Fresh or dried mint can be used to make a cup of delicious mint tea – just add water!

You can pick fresh mint from the garden, grow it on a windowsill or buy it in bunches from the supermarket. You will need three teaspoons of roughly-chopped fresh mint leaves for one cup of tea.

MAKING MINT TEA

1. Pop three teaspoons of roughly chopped mint leaves in a teapot, a jug or a special coffee pot that has a plunger. Pour freshly boiled water over the leaves (ask an adult for help when boiling water in a kettle).

2. Leave to 'infuse' for five minutes, before you strain and serve the tea.

DIY TEA BAGS

If you don't like having little bits of leaf floating in your tea, why not make your own tea bags? Cut a little square of muslin – measuring 10 cm by 10 cm. Place your herbs in the middle, then gather up the edges. Tie tightly with embroidery thread, leaving the ends long enough to let you dangle the tea bag in a cup.

HOW TO HAVE PERFECT POSTURE

Check your posture in a mirror and follow these dos and don'ts.

• **DO** hold your neck straight from your hairline to your shoulders.

• **DON'T** let your head jut forward and your neck curve. You should be able to balance a book on your head.

• **DO** relax your shoulders and keep your shoulder blades flat.

• **DON'T** let your chest cave inwards. Pull your shoulders out and back. Don't let them rise towards your ears.

• **DO** keep your spine straight with just a small curve in the small of your back, not a deep hollow.

- **DO** tuck in your bottom and pull in your stomach.

- **DON'T** let your feet splay outwards or inwards.

HOW TO SPOT A GENIUS

Ask a friend to count the number of Fs in the following text.

FINISHED FILES ARE
THE RESULT OF YEARS OF
SCIENTIFIC STUDY
COMBINED WITH THE
EXPERIENCE OF YEARS.

There are six Fs in the sentence, but most people only count three. This is because many people's brains don't register that the word 'OF' contains an F. Anyone who counts all six Fs on the first go is a genius.

HOW TO MAKE SURE YOUR TRAINERS SMELL REALLY GOOD

Here are some fool-proof ways of avoiding those embarrassing moments when you sit back, kick off your shoes and your friends kick up a fuss. These techniques are guaranteed to ensure you have the sweetest-smelling trainers around.

- Stuff unused tea bags into each shoe and leave for a couple of days.

- Sprinkle the inside of each trainer with talcum powder.

- Drip a couple of drops of essential oil on the inner soles. Try tea tree, rose or peppermint oil.

- Fill two clean socks with cat litter (ideally some that your cat hasn't already used), and leave them in your trainers overnight.

HOW TO MAKE HAND SHADOWS

Stun your friends and family with these amazing hand shadows.

To achieve the maximum 'Wow!' effect, perform your shadow show in a darkened room with a white or light-coloured wall. Aim a powerful desk lamp at the wall and position your hands in front of it. You could even get a friend in on the act.

spider   cat   dog

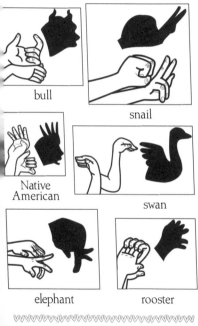

bull

snail

Native American

swan

elephant

rooster

HOW TO MAKE CHOCOLATE PECAN FUDGE

Create these simply delicious, chocolatey treats.

You Will Need:

- 450 g dark chocolate
- 75 g unsalted butter (at room temperature) • 400 g tin sweetened condensed milk
- ½ teaspoon vanilla essence
- 100 g of chopped pecan nuts
- baking parchment • 20-cm square baking tin

WHAT YOU DO

1. Heat the chocolate, butter and condensed milk together in a

saucepan over a low heat until the chocolate melts. Keep stirring and be careful not to let it burn. Get an adult to help so you don't singe your fingers.

2. Take the saucepan off the heat when the chocolate has melted and stir in the vanilla essence.

3. Stir in the chopped pecan nuts.

4. Line the baking tin with greased baking parchment. Then pour in the mixture.

5. Put the mixture in the fridge and leave it until it has completely set

6. Cut the fudge into bite-sized pieces, and wrap each piece in greaseproof paper until you're ready to eat it.

HOW TO SEND A MESSAGE IN MORSE CODE

In Morse code, each letter of the alphabet is made up of dots and dashes, the dots being short pulses and the dashes long pulses.

There are many ways you can send a message in Morse code.

The easiest method is to use a torch. Use the Morse code alphabet below to spell out your messages.

MORSE CODE ALPHABET

A	.—	J	.———	S	...
B	—...	K	—.—	T	—
C	—.—.	L	.—..	U	..—
D	—..	M	——	V	...—
E	.	N	—.	W	.——
F	..—.	O	———	X	—..—
G	——.	P	.——.	Y	—.——
H	....	Q	——.—	Z	——..
I	..	R	.—.		

HOW TO MAKE FRIENDS WITH A YETI

The Yeti is also known as the Abominable Snowman. Does the word 'abominable' worry you at all? Perhaps it should – especially bearing in mind a Yeti is said to be three metres tall and weigh about 600 kilograms. Moreover, a Yeti is very hairy, so it may not be a good companion for you if you suffer from pet allergies.

However, if you're quite sure you want to be best mates with this mythical creature, here's some advice.

• First, find your Yeti. This will not be easy. You need to travel to the Himalayan mountains of Nepal and Tibet. Bring plenty of warm clothes.

(The Yeti has thick fur to keep him warm.) There are reports of similar creatures in other parts of the world – you could try the Sasquatch in Canada, Bigfoot in America, Mapinguary in Brazil or Yowie in Australia.

• The Yeti is rarely seen so he must be very shy. Don't make any sudden movements, and try to look friendly and approachable. Be patient – it may be a long time before the Yeti decides you are friendly.

• Try tempting out your Yeti with food. Reports agree that the Yeti is an ape-like creature, so he will probably like bananas.

• Once you have charmed your Yeti, try interesting him in winter sports such as snowboarding, skiing or sledging. He may already be an expert, in which case he could teach you some impressive tricks.

• Speaking to your Yeti could be a problem – he may not speak English. In fact, he might be able to communicate only in chimp-like grunts and shrieks. You'll have to find other fun things to do together to make up for the lack of conversation. As well as winter sports, try toasting marshmallows over a campfire, star-gazing, or flying kites.

HOW TO COPE WITH HOMESICKNESS

Does being away from home make you want to curl up under a blanket and sob? Here's the inside story on how to cope when your pals, parents, and your own bed seem far away.

FAMILY FEELINGS

Before setting off on holiday, select

photos of your family and friends
and pop them in your suitcase.
When you get to your destination,
put them beside your bed. If you
really miss your folks in the night,
simply roll over to see their happy,
smiling faces beaming down at you.

Remember, it is easy to phone, write
to or email your family when you
need them. Why not decide on a set
time of day to contact your parents?
You can focus on this during any
wobbly moments.

BANISH THE BLUES

Fill your mind with positive thoughts.
Instead of thinking, 'If I was at home,
I could be cuddled up on the sofa
watching a DVD with my sister,' tell
yourself, 'I can watch a DVD any

time. Today I will do something new and exciting.'

Remind yourself that you are only away from home temporarily. When you get back, your bedroom, house and family will still be there. You should try to make the most of the changes to your routine that a holiday offers. To stay positive, write down the new experiences you are having in your diary. List at least three interesting things that happen to you each day. Adventures never happen to those who fear leaving the comfort of their own homes. Once you're back home and your mum is nagging you to tidy your room, you might just wish you could go away again!

PLAN AHEAD

Perhaps when you are blue, what you are really feeling is disappointment with your holiday. Maybe you have been looking forward to going away for ages, but are not having as much fun as you had hoped. You might confuse the empty feeling with homesickness. Make sure you plan something fun to do right away. It is important to change how you feel about your holiday while you can still enjoy it.

SHARE YOUR FEELINGS

If you really can't help missing the people back home, don't bottle up your feelings. Confide in someone. One of your friends might confess that they often feel homesick, too.

HOW TO PLAY CLOCK WATCHERS

All you need for this game is an alarm clock and three or more players. Make sure you cover up any other clocks in the room and confiscate all watches and mobile phones!

Get everyone to stand in a circle. Set the alarm clock so that it will ring in about two minutes' time. The idea is for each player to sit down when they think the alarm is going to ring – they should shout out their name as they sit down. The last person to sit down before the alarm rings is the winner and anyone left standing after it has rung must pay a forfeit.

HOW TO HIDE
YOUR DIARY

Follow these devious dos and don'ts to make sure your diary's secrets stay safe.

• **DO** make a 'decoy' – a fake diary that puts people off the trail of the real thing. Write the word 'DIARY' in big letters on a brightly coloured book and scribble some convincingly 'false' entries inside it. This should fool any snoopers into thinking it's the real deal.

• **DO** hide your diary inside another book when you want to write in it. If anyone asks what you are doing, you can pretend to be doing your homework.

• **DON'T** remove your diary from its hiding place unless you want to write in it. Never carry it around in your bag. If someone discovers it, your secrets will be literally 'out of the bag' in no time.

• **DON'T** hide your diary under your pillow – it's far too obvious. Instead, try tucking it inside the pocket of an old coat that you never wear. Hang it at the back of your wardrobe. No one will think to look there.

HOW TO BLOW THE BIGGEST BUBBLE

Put a piece of bubblegum in your mouth and chew it well. The larger the piece of gum, the larger the bubble you can blow. Make sure it is soft and stretchy.

With your tongue, flatten the gum across the backs of your top and bottom front teeth. With your tongue, push the centre of the gum out between your teeth. Seal your lips all around the bulge in the gum. Blow into the bulge of gum, and see how big your bubble gets before it pops!

HOW TO MAKE SENSE WHILE TALKING NONSENSE

'Oxymoron' is the name given to a figure of speech where two words or phrases that seem to contradict each other are put together. Oxymorons don't make any sense, but they make complete sense. Here are some to use:

- Pretty ugly
- Deafening silence
- Constant change
- Exact estimate
- Instant classic
- Liquid gas
- Advanced beginner
- Alone together

HOW TO DECODE THE SECRETS OF BODY LANGUAGE

Did you know that by examining the way someone uses their body, or their body language, it is sometimes possible to reveal the secrets of what they are thinking? Body language is a way we communicate without speaking. Some common gestures are decoded below.

MIRROR IMAGE

If someone mirrors your movements, it can mean they like you, and want to show they are similar to you.

It can also mean they feel a little nervous around you. Try to make them feel comfortable and at ease.

CROSSED ARMS

If someone has their arms crossed while you are talking to them, it could indicate that they are upset or angry with you. Beware what you say to them, as they might pick an argument with you at any moment.

HEAD TILT

Someone tilting their head is a subconscious way of showing they

aren't dangerous or threatening. The tilt can also mean that what is being said is a joke.

OPEN PALMS

If someone holds their palms facing

you while they are talking, it usually means that they are being open and honest. If they keep their palms apart, but their fingertips touching, this means they are trying to make you feel confident about what they are saying.

EYE CONTACT

Making eye contact – looking into someone's eyes – indicates that you feel comfortable around them. If someone  tries to avoid making eye contact with you, you should suspect they may be telling you fibs.

HOW TO FLOAT A FRIEND

This is an amazing trick. There's no real explanation for why or how it works – it just does. Find five friends willing to take part in your experiment. Choose one friend to be the subject who will be lifted, and ask her to sit on a chair.

Ask each of the other four girls to place their hands together, with their palms touching and their fingers outstretched.

One girl must place her fingers under the bent left knee of the subject on the chair. Another places her fingers in the same position under the right knee. The third girl places her fingers under one of the subject's armpits, and the fourth girl places their fingers under the other armpit.

Tell your friends to try to lift the person up from the chair. Chances are they will fail.

Next, ask everyone to stack their hands one on top of the other on top of the subject's head and lightly press down. Tell them to keep pressing while you count to ten, and on the count of ten to quickly get back into their lifting positions and try to lift again – it will work!

NOTE TO READERS

The publisher and author disclaim any liability
for accidents or injuries that may occur as a
result of the information given in this book.

You need to use your best common sense at all
times, particularly when heat or sharp objects are
involved, and follow safety precautions and
advice from responsible adults at all times.
Always wear appropriate safety gear, stay within
the law and local rules, and be considerate of
other people.